D1544652

SUPERSTARS OF WRESTLING

CM PUNK

By Ryan Nagelhout

Gareth Stevens
Publishing

Please visit our website, www.garethstevens.com. For a free color catalog of all our high-quality books, call toll free 1-800-542-2595 or fax 1-877-542-2596.

Library of Congress Cataloging-in-Publication Data

Nagelhout, Ryan.
  CM Punk / Ryan Nagelhout.
    p. cm. — (Superstars of wrestling)
  Includes index.
  ISBN 978-1-4339-8523-2 (pbk.)
  ISBN 978-1-4339-8524-9 (6-pack)
  ISBN 978-1-4339-8522-5 (library binding)
  1. CM Punk, 1978—Juvenile literature. 2. Wrestlers—United States—Biography—Juvenile literature. I. Title.
  GV1196.C25N34 2013
  796.812092—dc23
  [B]
                                    2012029063

First Edition

Published in 2013 by Gareth Stevens Publishing
111 East 14th Street, Suite 349
New York, NY 10003

Copyright © 2013 Gareth Stevens Publishing

Designer: Nicholas Domiano
Editor: Ryan Nagelhout

Photo credits: Cover background Denis Mironov/Shutterstock.com; cover, pp. 7, 13 Moses Robinson/Getty Images Entertainment/Getty Images; p. 5 Jim R. Bounds/AP Images for WWE; p. 9 Gaye Gerard/Getty Images Entertainment/Getty Images; p. 11 Miami Herald/McClatchy-Tribune/Getty Images; p. 15 Lisa Maree Williams/Getty Images Entertainment/Getty Images; p. 17 AP Images/Marc Serota; pp. 19, 21 Bob Levey/WireImage/Getty Images; p. 23 Kevin Mazur/WireImage/Getty Images; p. 25 Paul Abell/AP Images for WWE; p. 27 Jesse Grant/WireImage/Getty Images; p. 29 Marc Stamas/Getty Images Entertainment/Getty Images.

Printed in the United States of America

CPSIA compliance information: Batch #CW13GS: For further information contact Gareth Stevens, New York, New York at 1-800-542-2595.

Contents

Meet Punk

CM Punk is a WWE superstar!

Punk's real name is Phillip Jack Brooks. He was born on October 26, 1978. His family lived in Chicago, Illinois.

Growing Grappler

Punk started wrestling with his friends in Chicago. He quickly rose through the wrestling ranks and turned pro in 1999. The WWE was in his sights!

9

The "CM" in his name came from an early tag team match. It first stood for Chick Magnet!

Punk uses many different styles to wrestle. He has trained in kickboxing and a martial art called jujitsu.

13

On the Edge

CM Punk doesn't smoke, drink, or use any drugs. This is called Straight Edge, or living a clean lifestyle. He wants to be healthy!

Punk left Chicago to pursue his wrestling dreams. He worked with Ohio Valley Wrestling, NWA, and Ring of Honor. He was a star everywhere he went!

Big Start

Punk signed with the WWE in 2005.

In August 2006, he made his debut,

beating Justin Credible in an

ECW match.

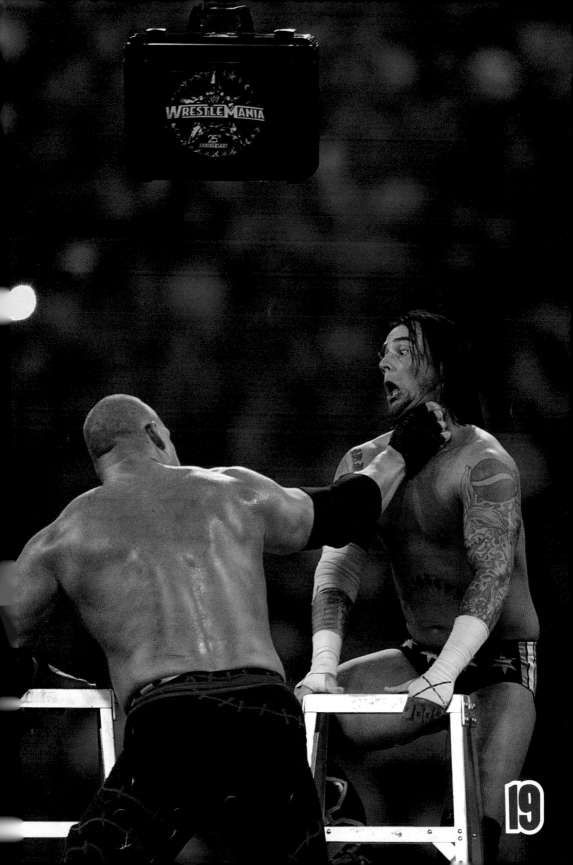

Punk got his first shot at a title in 2008. He beat six wrestlers in a Ladder match to win a "Money in the Bank" briefcase. This gave him a chance at his first title belt.

21

A Punk Crowned

In June 2008, Punk cashed in his briefcase for a title match. He beat Edge for his first World Heavyweight Championship. It was the first of many titles!

23

Triple Punk

Punk also won the World Tag Team title with Kofi Kingston in 2008 and the WWE title in 2009. The wins made him the nineteenth Triple Crown winner in WWE history!

25

Leaving So Soon?

On July 17, 2011, Punk reclaimed the WWE title from John Cena. Then he threatened to leave the WWE!

What's Next?

Punk later signed a new deal. This means CM Punk is here to stay!

What will he do next?

Timeline

1978	Punk is born Phillip Jack Brooks on October 26.
1999	Punk starts wrestling professionally.
2005	CM Punk signs with the WWE.
2006	Punk wins his WWE debut in August.
2008	Punk wins his first WWE title.
2009	Punk completes the WWE Triple Crown.
2011	Punk reclaims the WWE title. He threatens to leave the WWE.
	Punk signs new WWE contract in July.

For More Information

Books:

Fandel, Jennifer. *CM Punk: Straight Edge Heel.* North Mankato, MN: Capstone Press, 2012.

Shields, Brian. *CM Punk.* New York, NY: DK Publishing, 2009.

Smith, Tony. *CM Punk.* Minneapolis, MN: Bellwether Media, Inc., 2012.

Websites:

CM Punk
wwe.com/superstars/cmpunk
Check out the official WWE page for CM Punk.

The Official CM Punk Website
cmpunk.com
Keep up to date with the latest CM Punk news on his official site.

Glossary

briefcase: a flat case for carrying papers or books

championship: a contest to decide the overall winner

debut: a first official public appearance

jujitsu: Japanese art of fighting using only throws and holds

pursue: to follow or try to accomplish

Index